ROCKFORD PUBLIC LIBRARY

3 1112 018658621

P9-CBR-727

WITHDRAWN

J 741.51 EPP
Eppard, Jon
Manga

101912

ROCKFORD PUBLIC LIBRARY
Rockford, Illinois
www.rockfordpubliclibrary.org
815-965-9511

YOU CAN DRAW IT!
MANGA

ROCKFORD PUBLIC LIBRARY

WRITTEN BY JON EPPARD
ILLUSTRATED BY JOEL VOLLMER

BELLWETHER MEDIA · MINNEAPOLIS, MN

This edition first published in 2013 by Bellwether Media, Inc.

No part of this publication may be reproduced in whole or in part without written permission of the publisher.
For information regarding permission, write to Bellwether Media, Inc., Attention: Permissions Department,
5357 Penn Avenue South, Minneapolis, MN 55419.

Library of Congress Cataloging-in-Publication Data

Eppard, Jon.
  Manga / by Jon Eppard.
     pages cm – (You can draw it!)
  Includes bibliographical references and index.
  Summary: "Information accompanies step-by-step instructions on how to draw manga. The text level and subject matter
is intended for students in grades 3 through 7"–Provided by publisher.
  ISBN 978-1-60014-812-5 (hardcover : alk. paper) – ISBN 978-1-60014-857-6 (pbk. : alk. paper)
  1. Comic books, strips, etc.–Japan–Technique–Juvenile literature. 2. Cartooning–Technique–Juvenile literature. I. Title.
NC1764.5.J3E67 2012
741.5'1–dc23
                                            2012019352

Text copyright © 2013 by Bellwether Media, Inc. PILOT, EXPRESS, and associated logos are trademarks and/or
registered trademarks of Bellwether Media, Inc. SCHOLASTIC, CHILDREN'S PRESS, and associated logos are
trademarks and/or registered trademarks of Scholastic Inc.

Printed in the United States of America, North Mankato, MN.

TABLE OF CONTENTS

MANGA!

Manga is the Japanese form of comics and cartoons. The word itself means "whimsical drawings." Manga drawings are based on a style of **sketching** that was developed over 200 years ago in Japan. Today they tell stories of adventure, fantasy, science fiction, and more.

DRAWING FROM COMICS IS A GREAT PLACE
TO START. WORK YOUR WAY UP TO
DRAWING FROM YOUR IMAGINATION.

Before you begin drawing, you will need a few basic supplies.

PAPER

DRAWING PENCILS

2B OR NOT 2B?

NOT ALL DRAWING PENCILS ARE THE SAME. "B" PENCILS ARE SOFTER, MAKE DARKER MARKS, AND SMUDGE EASILY. "H" PENCILS ARE HARDER, MAKE LIGHTER MARKS, AND DON'T SMUDGE VERY MUCH AT ALL.

BLACK INK PEN

COLORED PENCILS
(ALL DRAWINGS IN THIS BOOK WERE FINISHED WITH COLORED PENCILS.)

ERASER

PENCIL SHARPENER

Girl Figure
The Fiery Fighter

Curves are emphasized in female characters, with hips often wider than the shoulders. Collarbones are also **pronounced**. Artists often use **posture** and stance to make female characters appear innocent or **passive**. Some characters break that mold. This girl warrior shatters it!

1

BEGIN WITH CIRCLES FOR THE HEAD, BODY, AND FEET

USE A STRAIGHT EDGE TO START THE LINES FOR THE SWORDS

BREAK IT DOWN

JUST ABOUT ANY SUBJECT YOU'RE DRAWING CAN BE BROKEN DOWN INTO SMALLER PARTS. LOOK FOR CIRCLES, OVALS, SQUARES, AND OTHER BASIC SHAPES THAT CAN HELP BUILD YOUR DRAWING.

2

DRAW THE OUTLINE OF THE CAPE, SWORDS, AND SHOULDER ARMOR

ADD SHAPES FOR LEGS

ADD THE MOUTH
AND EYES

3

DON'T FORGET
THE BELT

4

LIGHTLY DRAW DETAILS
ON THE ARMOR,
SWORDS, CAPE,
AND HAIR

5

INK AND COLOR

THIS WARRIOR HAS A BLACK SUIT,
RED CAPE, BRIGHT GREEN EYES, AND
FIERY HAIR. YOU WOULDN'T WANT TO
MESS WITH THIS FIRECRACKER!

Girl Portrait
The Wide-Eyed and Innocent

Look first at the **expressive** eyes. Females are often drawn with wide eyes and large pupils. **Highlights** within the pupils indicate a light source. Larger highlights are used to show innocence. Other defining features of female manga characters include full lips, a small nose, and a heart-shaped face.

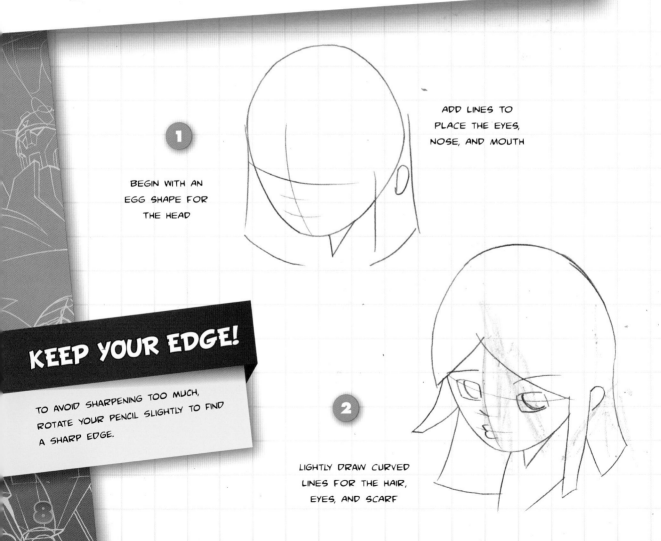

1 BEGIN WITH AN EGG SHAPE FOR THE HEAD

ADD LINES TO PLACE THE EYES, NOSE, AND MOUTH

2 LIGHTLY DRAW CURVED LINES FOR THE HAIR, EYES, AND SCARF

KEEP YOUR EDGE!

TO AVOID SHARPENING TOO MUCH, ROTATE YOUR PENCIL SLIGHTLY TO FIND A SHARP EDGE.

LIGHTLY ADD SHAPES
FOR THE HAIR SHINE

3

DRAW THE DETAILS OF
THE FACE AND SCARF

4

SHADE THE EYES
AND NECK

5

INK AND COLOR

BLUE EYES, RED LIPS, AND A
DEEP PURPLE SCARF MAKE THIS
GIRL A PERFECT MANGA BEAUTY!

9

Guy Figure
The Total Troublemaker

The male figure is defined by angles rather than curves. Shoulders are often broader than the hips, and muscles are emphasized. This character has both feet grounded in a wide stance. This common male pose displays power and aggression. Don't be fooled by the little stuffed bear. This kid is looking for trouble!

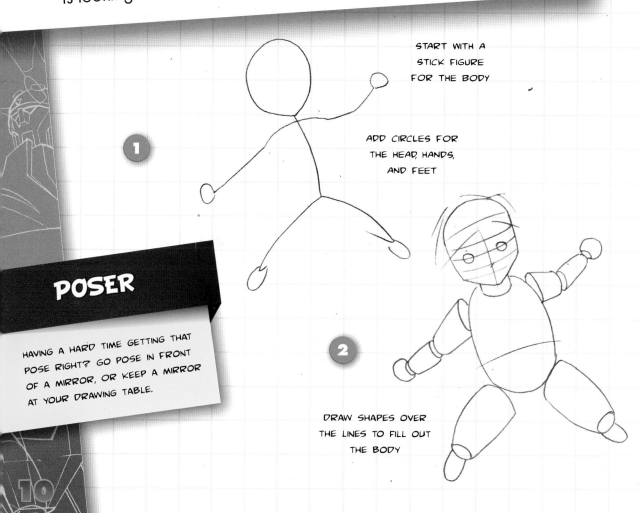

1

START WITH A STICK FIGURE FOR THE BODY

ADD CIRCLES FOR THE HEAD, HANDS, AND FEET

2

DRAW SHAPES OVER THE LINES TO FILL OUT THE BODY

POSER

HAVING A HARD TIME GETTING THAT POSE RIGHT? GO POSE IN FRONT OF A MIRROR, OR KEEP A MIRROR AT YOUR DRAWING TABLE.

ADD DETAILS TO THE
HAIR AND FACE

3

CONNECT SHAPES
WITH CURVED LINES

DON'T FORGET THE
TEDDY BEAR

4

ADD DETAILS TO
THE CLOTHES

5

INK AND COLOR

BLACK AND RED CLOTHES
HINT THAT THIS BOY IS ABOUT
TO MAKE MISCHIEF.

Guy Portrait
The Mystery Dude

The male character tends to have a long face and square chin. He often has a thicker neck and bigger nose than his female peers. His eyes, however, are smaller. Both pupils and highlights shrink to create a not-so-innocent expression. The eyes and smirk on this guy say that he's got something up his sleeve.

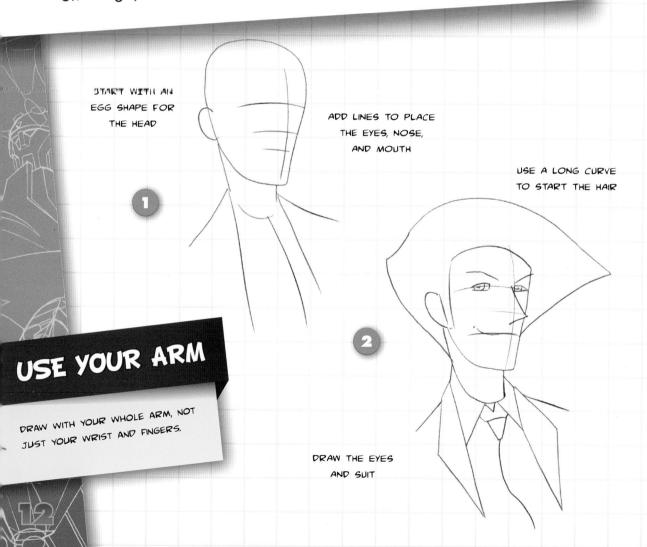

START WITH AN EGG SHAPE FOR THE HEAD

ADD LINES TO PLACE THE EYES, NOSE, AND MOUTH

USE A LONG CURVE TO START THE HAIR

1

2

DRAW THE EYES AND SUIT

USE YOUR ARM

DRAW WITH YOUR WHOLE ARM, NOT JUST YOUR WRIST AND FINGERS.

LIGHTLY DRAW DETAILS FOR
THE SUIT, HAIR,
AND EARS

3

FINISH THE
MESSY HAIR

4

SHADE UNDER
THE NECK

5

INK AND COLOR

MESSY BLACK HAIR, GREEN EYES,
AND A COOL GRAY SUIT ARE
ALL THIS GUY NEEDS TO LOOK
HIS FINEST.

13

Villain Figure
The Freak of Nature

Many manga villains are not human in origin. Instead they borrow parts from aliens, **demons**, robots, and critters. This evil-doer begins with a jelly bean shape. From there, **proportions** are not important. Just be sure that the final result is utterly creepy.

LIGHTLY DRAW LINES FOR THE ARMS, NECK, AND LEGS

1

BEGIN WITH A LARGE JELLY BEAN FOR THE BODY AND A CIRCLE FOR THE HEAD

2

PLACE SHAPES OVER THE LINES FOR THE ARMS, NECK, AND LEGS

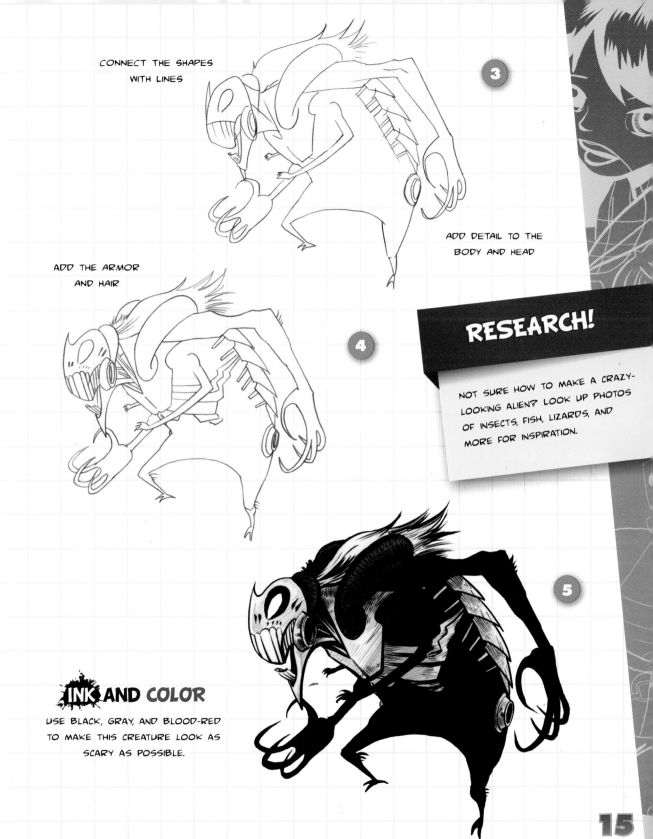

CONNECT THE SHAPES
WITH LINES

3

ADD DETAIL TO THE
BODY AND HEAD

ADD THE ARMOR
AND HAIR

4

RESEARCH!

NOT SURE HOW TO MAKE A CRAZY-LOOKING ALIEN? LOOK UP PHOTOS OF INSECTS, FISH, LIZARDS, AND MORE FOR INSPIRATION.

5

INK AND COLOR

USE BLACK, GRAY, AND BLOOD-RED TO MAKE THIS CREATURE LOOK AS SCARY AS POSSIBLE.

15

Villain Portrait
The Master of Mayhem

Villains take on many forms, but their evil look starts with the pairing of angry eyes and a vicious smile. This villain looks crazed and dangerous with his beady eyes and toothy grin. Sharp angles and a whacky headpiece complete this portrait of pure evil.

SMUDGE IT

SMUDGING YOUR PENCIL MARKS WITH A WET FINGER OR SMUDGE STICK WILL GIVE YOU A VARIETY OF GRAY TONES.

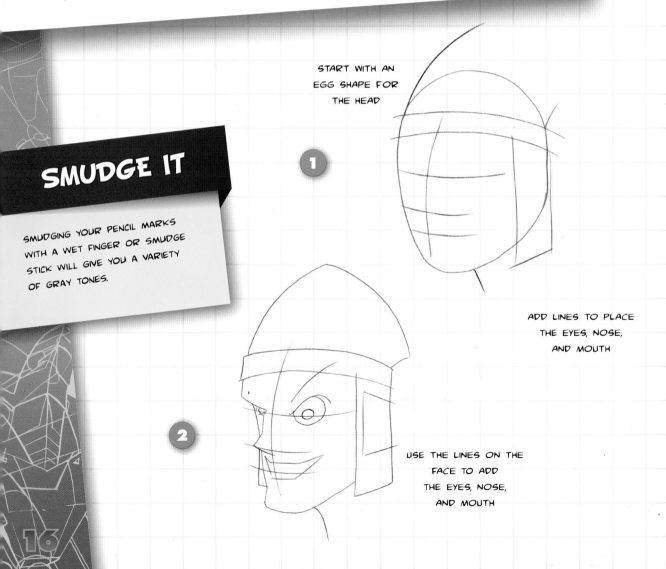

START WITH AN EGG SHAPE FOR THE HEAD

1

ADD LINES TO PLACE THE EYES, NOSE, AND MOUTH

2

USE THE LINES ON THE FACE TO ADD THE EYES, NOSE, AND MOUTH

LIGHTLY DRAW THE
FLAME-LIKE HAIR

3

4

ADD THE DETAILS TO
THE HEADPIECE, EYES,
NOSE, AND MOUTH

INK AND COLOR

GIVE THIS VILLAIN A NOT-OF-THIS-WORLD
LOOK WITH AN UNUSUAL SKIN TONE AND
HAIR COLOR!

5

Chibi
The Cutie

Chibi is a Japanese word meaning "small child." All chibi characters are meant to look cute and innocent. These qualities are shown through large, round heads and small bodies. Eyes are the most important feature in chibi characters. Pupils, **irises**, and eyebrows work together to express emotion. Mouths receive little detail, and noses are often left out.

BEGIN WITH A STICK FIGURE WITH A LARGE HEAD

1

LIGHTLY ADD THE FACIAL FEATURES

LIGHT TO DARK

BEGIN YOUR DRAWING WITH VERY LIGHT LINES. SLOWLY BUILD UP TO DARK LINES AS YOU REACH THE FINAL STEPS. THIS WILL ALLOW FOR EASY CORRECTION OF MISTAKES.

2

USE LARGE SHAPES TO ADD THE HAIR AND CLOTHES

ADD DETAILS TO THE
EYES AND HAIR

③

COMPLETE THE
PANTS, SCARF,
AND JACKET

④

INK AND COLOR

WITH BRIGHT PINK HAIR,
BIG EYES, AND A MATCHING PINK
SCARF, THIS CHIBI IS AS CUTE
AS THEY GET!

⑤

Mecha
The Supersized Humanoid

Mecha is a Japanese term meaning "mechanical." Robots and machines inspire this manga style. Layers of **geometric** shapes build the towering forms of supersized **humanoids**. Artists use **dual contour lines** to make drawings look three-dimensional. Light shading gives the **illusion** of a metallic shine. Details such as **rivets**, vents, and wires are important finishing touches.

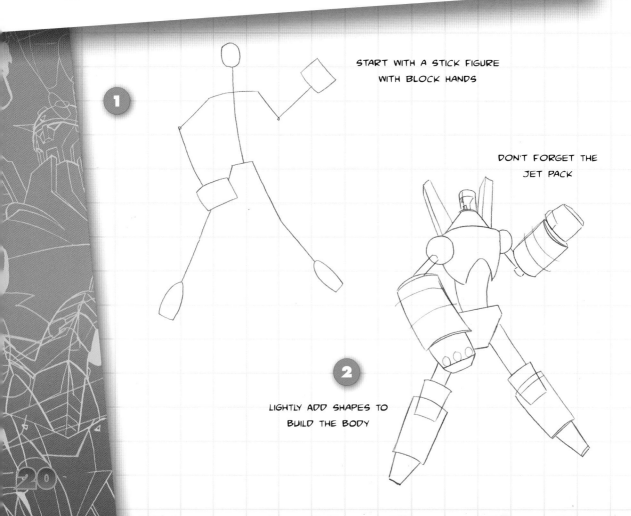

1

START WITH A STICK FIGURE
WITH BLOCK HANDS

DON'T FORGET THE
JET PACK

2

LIGHTLY ADD SHAPES TO
BUILD THE BODY

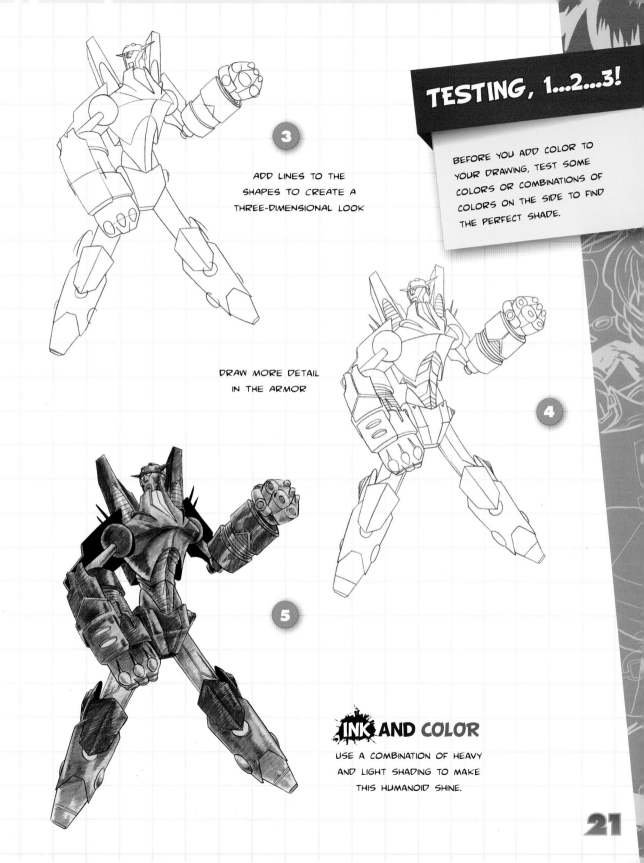

3

ADD LINES TO THE
SHAPES TO CREATE A
THREE-DIMENSIONAL LOOK

DRAW MORE DETAIL
IN THE ARMOR

BEFORE YOU ADD COLOR TO
YOUR DRAWING, TEST SOME
COLORS OR COMBINATIONS OF
COLORS ON THE SIDE TO FIND
THE PERFECT SHADE.

4

5

INK AND COLOR

USE A COMBINATION OF HEAVY
AND LIGHT SHADING TO MAKE
THIS HUMANOID SHINE.

21

GLOSSARY

demons—evil spirits

dual contour lines—double outlines that give a drawing a three-dimensional look

expressive—showing feeling

geometric—based on simple lines, circles, and squares

highlights—bright spots that are the reflection of a light source

humanoids—nonhumans that take on a human form

illusion—a false sense

irises—the colored portions of the eyes

passive—tending not to take an active role

posture—the way a person carries or positions his or her body

pronounced—strongly represented

proportions—the size of body parts in relation to one another and to the whole body

rivets—metal bolts used to fasten two pieces of material together

sketching—rough drawing or outlining

TO LEARN MORE

At the Library

Crilley, Mark. *Mastering Manga with Mark Crilley*. Cincinnati, Ohio: Impact, 2012.

Hart, Christopher. *Manga for the Beginner Chibis: Everything You Need to Start Drawing the Super-Cute Characters of Japanese Comics*. New York, N.Y.: Watson-Guptill Pub., 2010.

Takarai, Saori. *Manga Moods: 40 Faces + 80 Phrases*. Saitama, Japan: Japanime Co. Ltd., 2006.

On the Web

Learning more about manga
is as easy as 1, 2, 3.

1. Go to www.factsurfer.com.

2. Enter "manga" into the search box.

3. Click the "Surf" button and you will see a list of related Web sites.

With factsurfer.com, finding more information is just a click away.

INDEX